To Teresa and Peter, my great friends.

Acknowledgements

To Howard, ever patient and tactful for his suggestions.

To Andrew, for checking and his ability to summarise my waffle.

To Martin, my rock.

To "Scottish Shortbread Ann".

To all of Peter's Facebook followers for their encouragement and suggestions for a title for this collection (although we didn't use any of your suggestions!)

Cover Artwork: *Original artwork by Sheila Marsh (sheila@opustrg.co.uk)*

Layout & Design: *Daniel Ruffles*

Landscape Photography: *Daniel Ruffles (danielianphotography.com)*

Additional Photography: *Charmian Berry*

Walk With Me

Musings Through The Dementia Fog

Peter Berry & Deb Bunt

Original Photography from Daniel Ruffles

It has been almost a year since the publication of "Slow Puncture" and, inevitably, many things have changed. We have all lived through and, indeed, are still living through the pandemic, a period which, in turn, annoyed, baffled, confused, distressed, frightened and irritated us. I suspect many of us have been touched by a bereavement or a personal tragedy relating to COVID. And for many, the scandal around care homes and the emotional fall-out rumbles on. It has been hard for everyone; we have all had our grief and sorrows to endure and our patience has been stretched to its limits.

Peter, in common with many people who are living with dementia, told me that he has found it confusing and, probably, just that little bit harder than others. Not only did he have to learn new rules, the frequency with which they seemed to change and the uncertainty around those changes made it doubly difficult. But he felt it would be harder still when we finally emerged from lockdown because he would have to re-learn and remember people whom he had not seen for over a year. And, in July, when we were granted 'Freedom Day', this certainly seemed to be the case.

The pandemic is a global issue, one which touches us all, and it coincided with the publication of "Slow Puncture." On a more parochial level, the impositions of the COVID restrictions threw Peter and me off our guard and our planned promotional events had to be cancelled. However, despite this disappointment, we found there were still some unexpected pleasures which our book journey yielded which delighted and lifted us all. I think it's fair to say that, amidst the choppy waters created by COVID, we have managed to bob along on a gentle wave created by the "Slow Puncture" social media publicity.

Neither Peter nor I expected "Slow Puncture" to have been as well received as it has been - albeit in its own niche section - or to have prompted the creation of several podcasts, book group chats, newspaper articles, blogs and radio interviews as it has done.

It is true to say that knowing Peter has not only increased my knowledge of the countryside, of animals, of birds and of cycling (and enhanced my innate proclivity to pick up random injuries), it has given purpose to my retirement.

This is a book dedicated to Peter's poetry but first it feels appropriate to touch briefly upon three main areas of our relationship: friendship, trust and learning.

FRIENDSHIP

My friendship with Peter has allowed me to grow and develop into, I hope, a better person - someone more given to enjoying the moment rather than always wanting to rush on. And, of course, it is through Peter that I achieved my ambition of becoming an author. This friendship is very much a two-way street and I have benefited enormously from Peter's philosophy and actions.

It has been a wonderful journey and I can't explain how much the publication of the book and the resulting activities has meant. My friendship with Peter has thrown open the door to achieve my only real career objective and enabled me to say, "Reader: I am an author". Knowing Peter has put a firmer shape around the rather amorphous form which I lugged to Suffolk with me; my friendship with Peter has allowed a better version of me to emerge from the cynical and world weary me which, in retrospect, came across at times in "Slow Puncture."

We have met many people who are fascinated by Peter and his story; ours is a small community and we are often greeted by cheery waves or joyful recognition, particularly when Peter is riding his penny farthing. Not so long ago, we randomly met a young man called Daniel Ruffles whose photography of the Suffolk coastal area attracted my attention. When I looked at Daniel's photos I was strangely moved; his images tugged at my soul, and this planted the seed of an idea for me. This, in turn, grew into a collaboration: Peter's words and Daniel's photography bound together by their shared love of Suffolk.

Inevitably, as the last year progressed, Peter's memory has deteriorated. Teresa tries to allay her fears but they are never far away. This makes me remember Peter's words of three years ago when we discussed his 'dementia monster': *"Teresa has her own dementia monster: it's me."* That monster continues to stalk the corridors of the Berrys' house and bumps into Teresa more frequently than anyone would like to see.

Peter recognises that *"Teresa sees my failings, and I don't. She can*

3

measure the changes and I am not aware of them." Of course, there always were going to be changes and a deterioration in Peter's abilities. I consider myself fortunate in that I get the best of Peter: no more so that when he is on a bike, pedalling through the Suffolk lanes and away from the dementia monster, as he regales me with anecdotes of Suffolk characters whose names always have an unlikely ring to them (and I still suspect he sometimes makes them up to amuse me) and which always add to the joy of the narrative. In short, I get the best of Peter when he is just being Peter. Teresa sees the evening version of him: tired of mind, fuzzy memories, grey around the edges, the colour seeping away. This is the time that the dementia monster leans heavily on his shoulder, puffing out its ugly cheeks to create a fog through which Peter struggles to see with any clarity.

"Well, it is a progressive disease," Peter explains to me patiently but with a slight twinkle in his eye, as if it is I who has forgotten he is living with dementia. *"It's not going to get any better. Of course, I am less able to do some things. But for every door that closes, I find another one to push open. For every problem, I will continue to find a solution."* His mood remains bullish. It always will.

In the last year I have taken more time to reflect on Peter and his dementia monster. I have thought about what it might be like to stand in the shoes of someone who knows he is living with a progressive, terminal condition. Perhaps I do now have the faintest inkling of what that might be like, certainly more than I did before I came to Suffolk. But I do know that my knowledge is limited. No one's shoes really fit another person well enough to enable them to stand in them for long.

However, the one area I do understand so much better is my friendship with Peter. Although I alluded to it in "Slow Puncture" it is surely this, more than anything else, that moved me.

There is a brief section in the book on the nature of our friendship, which hints at what has since become so pivotal for me:

"It's very strange," says Peter. *"I have known you for over a year now and*

yet I don't know you. I don't really know anything about you. I'm sure you've told me, but I have no idea what you were like as a teenager, what it was like growing up, if your parents are alive, what your relationships have been like, what you did for a job; it's like you're a stranger. And yet, and yet… I feel very connected to you emotionally."

Friendship can be exposing and yet this exposure is just one way. So, whilst I know many of Peter's stories and adventures and can probably now complete many of these anecdotes for him, such is the capacity of my memory, each time Peter and I meet, it's as if I am a shadowy stranger, full of potential intrigue and mystery. And yet I am also so very familiar to him. I can't imagine what that must be like and the thought makes me slightly uncomfortable, as it has only now dawned on me that this is the case.

"I just have to use some instinct or my heart to know if I can trust people," he says, *"because I can't base my feelings on facts anymore. And that makes some of us with dementia quite vulnerable emotionally, don't you think?"*

When I wrote this section of "Slow Puncture", it was almost as an afterthought because I had a self-imposed deadline to meet. I was so keen to publish the book whilst Peter was able to appreciate its publication that I rather glossed over this area. I wish now I had taken more time to reflect on the enormity of Peter's words and how they have shaped our friendship.

Peter's lack of memory means we can't have that usual catch up that most friends do and so, by necessity, our friendship - and specifically his friendship towards me - is based on the here and now, his emotional instincts and responses.

Some time ago, Peter told me of an incident with his father which had happened fifty years ago. When I expressed surprise at how vivid that story and its memories were, he thumped his chest and said, *"I keep old memories, safe in the vault that not even dementia can unlock."*

I assume that this is how he functions with relationships and friendships. His sense of me is stored in his heart and whilst the finer details might not be accessible, the sense of who I am has been distilled from the murky liquid of his dementia. It is hoarded carefully and guarded zealously in his emotional safe.

Of course, this potentially could make ours an entirely one-sided friendship. And yet it is not. Throughout the book I stress that the relationship is one of mutual reciprocity, with Peter giving as much to me as I do to him. Of course, I have to repeat many things to Peter which he hears and processes only in that moment. So, when he asks if my parents are alive and I have told him dozens of times that they are not, does it matter that I have to tell him again? Probably not as much as it matters to Peter because on some deep, instinctual level, he must know he has asked me these questions. I imagine this must be immensely frustrating for him.

With the imposition of social distancing and the necessity to stay at home, I have spent time reflecting on how those with memory loss might be more emotionally vulnerable, how open to exploitation they might be and how utterly frightening it must be to live with this imbalance. And I think about our friendship and I hope - no, I know - that Peter feels safe and contained within its lopsided embrace.

Peter says he feels our friendship as if it is *"etched in his heart in bold letters"* and whilst he acknowledges that he is out of the loop for the minutiae of daily living, he has learned to deal with this. Peter knows the value of a friendship even if he does not know the layers of superficiality which encase it; he knows that what nestles under those layers is something worth preserving. And isn't that what's most important about friendship? That it means something? And no one will argue with Peter that our friendship does not mean something.

And because I do remember what Peter says, I know enough about his routine to understand that by the early evening he is generally tired of mind. I can visualise him at his home: there he sits, on the settee, with the wood burner blazing, accompanied on one side by a wistful sense of melancholia and on the other by his dementia monster, rubbing its warty fingers together, waiting to prod Peter.

And this is usually when Peter sends me one of his thoughts which he dictates through his phone if he is not able to type them. I do not want these musings to disappear into the dementia fog. Peter has breathed life into his thoughts and set them free. I want to keep these thoughts alive for him and for Teresa.

Some time ago, I received this message:
"Here I sit after a cycle ride on the sofa in silence next to my dementia monster. My escape was short but very fruitful. His and my silence is the proof of that. Acceptance and contentment are mine again."

One day last week, Peter and I cycled about forty miles. We spent a large chunk of the day in each other's company. In the evening Peter texted me:
"What have you been up to today, then?"

I remembered his earlier message about his acceptance and contentment and I hoped he was content now because I felt sad for him that our day, and all its fun, had been gobbled up by his ever-hungry monster.

When I told him that we had been cycling, he sent little laughing emojis back to me and, in the way that Peter has of diffusing sadness with humour, he texted:
"Well, I'm a knob."
"Your dementia is a knob," I texted back feeling defensive for my friend.

And then he sent this:
"But we had a good day, didn't we? And I will continue to build castles out of the rubble of my dementia."

And, as ever, I am touched that I have managed to creep across the drawbridge and that there is a small space inside his castle for me. And there I will sit, with my back to the wall, hugging my knees. I am his friend and it doesn't matter that Peter knows so little about me in his head because I know that he knows so much about me in his heart. As I sit, I know that Peter is gripping the key to the castle and to the vault; he will not relinquish

7

it and I am safe in the knowledge that our friendship is being vigilantly guarded from the gnashing, chomping jaws of the dementia monster who insists on roaming the draughty castle rooms.

TRUST

Peter willingly shares his fears and thoughts about his condition. He remains a showman, there is no question of that: he still puts on his showman's smile, albeit a somewhat hollow smile at times. He will still bluff and blag his way through a conversation but he is slowly coming to the realisation that it's sometimes too much to fight it. He has admitted as much, he needs to let it drift, to focus on what he can manage, not to struggle with what he cannot.

As Peter has said, Teresa is tied to him by emotional bonds which are hard to sever, whereas I am just connected to him through the flimsier ropes of friendship. That's not to say I don't care, but inevitably it impacts me less than it does Teresa.

And so, I am happy to be the recipient of his fears if it helps him and also protects Teresa. But the trust has had to be built, layer by careful layer, and I am touched that we have managed to do just that. Peter will not remember what he has told me. Like everything else, what he says to me is done in the moment and he will probably know he has told me something but won't know what it is. That scares me somewhat. Most of us dole out our inner fears carefully, giving great consideration to how much of our vulnerable under-belly we expose. Certainly, I tend to reflect on what I have said for days afterwards. But this cannot be the case for Peter.

I wonder how this trust has developed; what were its foundations? Is this trust a different type of trust than those without memory impairment may experience? What if he shares something with me, in the moment, and forgets? It does mean that he has lightened his load and that's a good thing. But it also means, in all likelihood, I am unlikely to forget.

I can only conclude that the trust runs deep, and is embedded in a crevice in Peter's heart, the place where he locks and preserves his emotional responses to life.

When I researched "trust in dementia", a range of techniques and strategies were thrown up but they all seemed to relate to how carers should inculcate trust with their charges/partners. None seemed to apply to Peter's intrinsic, emotional trust in me. I read of the necessity to speak clearly and slowly, to use short sentences, to give the person time to respond, to give them simple choices and to avoid creating complications. And certainly, having listened to Peter for the last three years, I would say it is particularly important not to over-complicate choices. All of this advice is undoubtedly true and relates, perhaps, to people further down the dementia journey than Peter is at this point.

However, I still don't think I am any clearer about the emotional intelligence required to build and maintain trust. Perhaps it doesn't matter. Perhaps all that matters is that Peter trusts me. And the other side to that is, of course, that I trust Peter. The trust is everything; analysing it will not offer an explanation. It's just there, something that we have created and has now taken root; it is something which has grown as the friendship has grown and, to use a tree analogy which will surely please Peter, the tiny bud of the acorn has grown into an oak tree and is immovable, unshakeable and constant. And there we can sit, together, under its leafy shade and take refuge from the dementia storm which is gathering apace in the distance.

LEARNING

The last couple of years have also taught me that I am still learning. I am neither the aficionado nor the authority on dementia, and I am certainly not the expert on Peter's condition. This is partly because - despite our friendship, and the trust we have built - he still protects me and only gives me limited access into that arena where his fears lie. The landscape Peter allows me to wander into is still relatively well maintained. He will not let me see the vaster, bleaker landscape where his fears have taken root and are growing, like unwieldly and unmanageable weeds, in his mind.

But the realisation that I know so little still has the capacity to shock me. Two contrasting and recent episodes come to mind: the first is an example of how I let complacency over-rule my knowledge; the second is how Peter's teaching enabled me to deal with a situation in a positive way.

Peter recently bought a new bike. This has gears and has meant Peter has had to re-learn the art of changing up and down the gears. He had got used to the single speed bike and so any change was going to present some difficulty.

The other day, when we were standing by our bikes, ready to go on a ride, a mutual acquaintance came over to us.

"How is Peter getting on with the new bike?" she asked. Her interest was genuine. But she asked me, not Peter. I compounded this by answering,

"Oh fine. It's a good bike. And he's remembering the gear changes really well."

And, as soon as I said it, I was furious with myself. The correct response, the decent response would have been to have said,

"Well, he's standing right here, why don't you ask him?"

A smile would have defused any perceived aggression. But I waded in and answered for a man whose verbal capacity remains unsurpassed! How am I meant to 'educate' people, when the ability to remain so ignorant, so thoughtless, still exists in me?

We cycled off and, as is my wont, I brooded for a few miles. Then, even though I knew Peter would have forgotten meeting this person and the ensuing conversation, I still felt compelled to apologise to him. I probably should have left it well alone but the scab was there, flapping as we cycled and it needed to be removed. It just had to be done even though this meant regaling him with the story (was that wrong to remind him that he had forgotten about the incident?) and then apologising to him for answering on his behalf. My conscience demanded it, even though common sense probably should have prevailed.

Peter was fine about it, of course he was. But it proved to me that, despite my belief that I know about dementia, I am still naïve, I can still fall into the trap as easily as the next person. It proved that I can never - and must never - stop learning.

Having beaten myself up about my thoughtlessness over this incident, I can now pat myself on the back over another incident where I believe I acted in congruence with Peter's dementia.

In June I had a fall, a clumsy silly fall, and I twisted my ankle. At one point, I feared it was broken because I couldn't put any weight on it. I told Peter and he was concerned. He said he would text the next day to see how I was.

"I will remember tomorrow…it's a chum thing," he reassured me.

And, sure enough, the next morning, I received his text:
"I know it's early but I had to know how you are."

I told him I was fine, much better and slightly embarrassed for making such a fuss about it.

Barely an hour later, Peter texted again.
"Morning, how's you?"

It was an easy decision to answer as if this was his first message; I did not tell him we had had this conversation barely sixty minutes earlier. What would have been the point?

"*I'm much better,*" I texted.

But then he texted, "*Shit, we've done that bit apparently*".
"*I honestly don't mind,*" I texted back, "*I know you forgot. OR you could say you remembered twice.*"
"*That's it, I remembered twice…thank you for that, that's my kind of thinking…*"

And there we are, I had learned a strategy from the master of strategies! I managed to make a positive out of a negative and that dovetailed with Peter's mindset and I imagine that it cemented a little more of the trust that we already had in each other.

The other thing I am still learning, and have only recently discovered, is that Peter has not read a book since he left school. Of course, he cannot read now in any meaningful way (he can read words but cannot read more than a sentence before he has forgotten what he's read) but before the onset of dementia he said would rather be doing than reading, rather be looking at instructions than immersing himself in fiction. I find this extraordinary because I find Peter's words to be profound and beautifully expressed. I consider Peter to be a poet, much more so than I could ever be. Oh, I can waffle on, I can wax lyrical and insert complex words into my prose but I am not so sure I have the seemingly natural flair for spontaneously expressing myself so perfectly as Peter has.

Peter still has the capacity to surprise me, to make me catch my breath and I suppose I have learned never to assume that I know everything; I must always listen and learn because I believe Peter has much more to teach me.

So, those are the pressing things on which I have brooded and reflected since "Slow Puncture" was published. Which brings me back to friendship and to the poetry which Peter sends me by text in the evenings. I look forward with a mixture of pleasure and trepidation to the musings I receive. I know he sends them to me because he trusts me and because our friendship has created a safe space for him to do so. I know he does not wish to weigh Teresa down with his thoughts, but equally he wants his thoughts to be wrapped up and preserved for him.

I see Peter's poetry as a gift: it symbolises so much more than the workings of his tired mind. It reflects trust, honesty and friendship. It is all of those things encapsulated in a few lines, generated by a weary mind.

Over the last year or so I have collated Peter's early evening text messages, and both he and Teresa have been happy for me to do so. Peter says he does not want those words *"lost to the tides of dementia"*; he wants them *"written in stone"* in the same way I wrote his story in stone. The giving and receiving of the poems and thoughts is a precious gift, given with a generous and open heart by Peter and received with, perhaps, the faintest trace of sorrow, by me. Because, whilst I see every poem as a gift, there is also the recognition that it is something which has chiselled away a little more from Peter's brain. It is not a tainted gift, far from it, but it is a gift, inevitably, sheathed in a layer of sadness.

As I said earlier, the photos accompanying the poems are from Daniel Ruffles. I couldn't think of a better accompaniment to Peter's words than these photographs of Suffolk. Suffolk is Peter's home, where his heart is; the countryside brings his mind to life and stirs up old memories. When I think of Suffolk, I immediately think of Peter and I know that I will always do so.

I think Peter's words are beautiful. They are raw and in the moment; their beauty is in their stark simplicity. They are not pretentious and they were not intended for analysis or for submission for literary critique. Peter has not studied the mechanics or rules of poetry, he knows nothing of syntax, verse or rhymed iambic pentameter couplets (nor, indeed, do I; and yes, I did have to google the rules of poetry). Peter did not spend hours composing, editing or refining his words. What you see in the following pages are his immediate thoughts and fears and, quite often, his fist shaking defiance. They are thoughts shared with me and captured by me, for Peter, for my friend. As Peter himself has said, *"When I hit enter, the information disappears; you are my 'plug in and save' device."*

What follows on these pages is my tribute to our friendship, the best plug in and save device that I can offer him.

Peter arrives in style for a talk at Saxmundham library

Peter makes a point during his talk at Saxmundham library

September 2019-
December 2019

SHELTERING FROM THE STORM

Dementia is stripping me of myself but I have become more than I ever was.
We build our own shelters from the storm that is dementia
because others do not realise how strong it has to be.
But it will soon be lost to the tide of dementia, swept away by the dark sea.
I walk a narrow, rocky, dark dementia path that demands 110% of me
not to stumble
because if I fall, I fear I shall not stand again.
My life with dementia has become a book with one page
But that page is constantly formed and re-written,
The erased memory is followed by the created and embraced now.

IN MY WORLD

*In my world with dementia, today is not just a new day but my first day of the
week and the first day for a long time.
The moment has become the moment,
just the moment.
I am the now
and the now is me.*

ONE WAY STAIRCASE

Dementia is like a staircase:
the steps up are not the same size
and sometimes you step further than you like.
The stair case is one-way only
and it's difficult, so difficult, to go back up.

MY TOMORROWS ARE STILL MINE

Dementia sits on my shoulder,
whispers in my ear and takes my yesterdays and my todays
but my tomorrows are still mine.
Write it down so it is always my tomorrow.

SHADOWS

Dementia shadows are often long and dark at the end of a bright day.
A weary mind is a slow mind.
Hopefully tomorrow shall be bright and clear and dementia's shadows will be
short and light.
From the dark shadow of my dementia
there is light and hope for others.
The beacon in my mind does not always shine on an empty waste land,
it shines on new growth like a fire-stricken forest coming back to life.

MEMORIES

How strange it is to have a memory outside of my head.
It soon goes but you have it for me always.
That's strange.

THE BLACK HOLE

It's like I'm a small planet in a big solar system with many other bigger planets
surrounding me;
I'm getting smaller.
Dementia is the black hole in my solar system,
everything that enters it is gone.

WARRIORS

Dementia leans heavy on our shoulders and that makes it difficult to stand tall.
We shine on the outside like towering, beautiful lights for all to see
and yet inside we are dark and dull,
suppressing the shadows is what we do and we do it so very well.
We are all warriors.
All of us.

MY ESCAPE

Here I sit after a cycle ride on the sofa in silence next to my dementia monster.
My escape was short but very fruitful.
His and my silence is the proof of that.
Acceptance and contentment are mine again.

UNPREDICTABLE DEMENTIA

Unpredictable dementia.
Some days I walk tall, straight and strong
and other days I'm weak, bent over and old,
like living with a wild-eyed horse.
Uncontrollable, unpredictable dementia.
Dementia is my nothing
and my nothing is coming towards me.

MY THOUGHTS

Dementia:
the spider in the web of my mind;
my thoughts are flies
caught and waiting to be trapped and devoured by the dementia spider.
He's always hungry,
so hungry.
Dementia:
My thoughts are like the morning mist that disappear with the rising sun.
Beautiful whilst it lasts but gone,
leaving no trace of its existence.
My thoughts are like sand through my fingers.
My only hope is that they are saved by others and panned as if looking for gold,
the precious metals
that are my memories.

January 2020-
March 2020

DANCE FOR LIFE

I have learned to walk hand in hand with Alzheimer's
without letting its grip become too hard.
I have learned to try to warm its cold clasp,
softening its hold.
Walking alongside Alzheimer's is an art.
Trying not to stand its shadow,
we become dancers in a dance for life.

STANDING TALL AND STRONG

We with dementia are like elaborate clocks.
We stand proud with a face that never changes from year to year
but inside gears and springs are missing.
Standing tall and strong, others smile in our presence as they pass.
Broken we might be
but we have a purpose still.

THE DAILY GAME OF LIFE

Memories are like naughty children
playing hide and seek in the dementia garden,
running and laughing, they hide in the shadows of my mind.
"Come and find us," they call.
It's a game I sometimes win but more often than not I lose but must still play. The
days I win are clear and good,
the days I lose are dull and foggy.
The daily game of life.

April 2020-
July 2020

THE BITTER TASTE

Dementia is a rocky uneven path of treacle that I walk daily,
some days thick and sticky,
some days soft and smooth
but never sweet and nice tasting.
Dementia, the bitter taste in my mind.

THE HIDDEN MONSTER

Dementia, the hidden monster:
I walk like you,
I talk like you,
I laugh and joke with you.
You see someone who's doing so well
but yet in my mind a monster does dwell.
He is very hungry and lives very well.
His favourite food is the memories I make,
Taking from me every day
In so many different ways
And yet you do not see my monster
because he hides himself so very well.

CLOSING DOORS

My mind is a tower block:
My dementia is the lift.
It only works sometimes and stops at different floors.
Sometimes the doors open fully and so I can get out,
the other times the doors just slightly open so I can peer out,
I see a little glimpse of what might be there
Then the doors close,
To the next floor I go
My dementia whispering in my ear, step out if you dare
Faster and faster, it goes
What floor it will stop at, I will never know.

BUTTERFLIES

*My thoughts are like butterflies dancing in the breeze, trying to catch them is
something I can't do with ease;
the more I chase, the faster they get
I just can't get them all in my net.
They love to fly free and do their thing
All of my thoughts, not in my head, but on the wing.*

September 2020-
December 2020

IN THE EYE OF THE DEMENTIA STORM

I stand in the eye of my dementia storm,
trying to focus on the thoughts that circle me,
faster and faster, they twist,
as I reach out and grab them they turn to dust and are gone,
and yet I stand in the eye of the dementia storm,
safe and calm and happy
as always.

THE SILENT NOTHING

Dementia, the silent nothing, creeping like a dark shadow across the landscape of my mind, nowhere to shelter, nowhere to hide.
Dementia, the nothing, leaves nothing behind.

On days like this, dementia has a nasty bite, taking big lumps out.
On nice days dementia can only nibble a bit,
very small bits that I don't even notice.
On days like this, dementia is the garden shed in my mind filled with cobwebs and dust.
I cycle, so the shed is tidy and clean, everything is in order but the dementia spiders will spin their webs and catch my thoughts like flies and devour them, slowly.
And tomorrow, it begins again.
The silent nothing.

THE MONSTER

Dementia empties my head.
It is hungry and must be fed;
always demanding my thoughts.
I cycle to starve this monster.
I cycle to keep him thin;
I cycle so many miles
and yet he stays in my head with a big grin.

THE ANVIL

Some days dementia is a feather on my shoulders,
a quick puff and it flutters to the ground;
lately dementia is an anvil
that I have to carry, that I can't puff away.

WALK WITH ME

Walk with me in the gallery of my mind,
Where hang rows of pictureless frames.
Where blank canvasses are now
Were once colourful portraits when my life began.
My portraits are now created every day
and then brushed away
with a single dementia brush stroke.

January 2021-
July 2021

DEMENTIA SEA

My dementia sea, unstoppable but not uncontrollable.
Some of my memories are written in the sands on the dementia shore line and are
washed away on every high tide.
Some of my memories are written in the rocks and cliffs to weather the dementia
storms for many years to come.
I stand with my back to the sea, smiling at my rock memories
then I climb up and chisel them a little deeper,
making them last forever.
Dementia, unstoppable,
but not uncontrollable.

THE HUMMING BIRD

When I sit my memories are like moths fluttering near the lamp,
tired and confused;
when I cycle my memories become humming birds,
fast and focused, feeding on the nectar around me,
giving me the energy for life.

INCLUDE ME

I hear everything, I see everything, I understand everything,
but I forget.
Don't let me be forgotten,
if you do then my dementia has won,
help me win the race,
run with me,
include me.

ABOVE THE MIST

I wish I could fly high above the mist,
up in the clear sky away from the dementia smog,
the mist, the fog that's engulfing my mind.

Dementia's tide of change,
it erodes the shores of my mind,
changing my landscape with every wave,
I build defences to live behind,
strong and stable in my mind,
I must keep building to stem the tide
but dementia keeps taking my mind.
But I will continue to build castles out of the rubble of my dementia.

BLANK CANVAS

Sometimes I realise that my life is a blank canvas that is repainted every day in
wonderful colours
only to be taken down from the galleries of my mind
and then rehung the next day in a different location
It's a funny old world I live in.

CYCLING ABOVE THE DIRTY MIST

Cycling is the fuel that runs my engine,
the oil that lubricates my mind
the master of my dementia,
the ringmaster that
Tames my monster to make him perform for me,
the key to my dementia shackle,
life is sweet when I cycle
and bitter when I'm not.
Cycling is like a balloon that takes me high into the sky, far above the dirty mist of
dementia.
Up here I can breathe and think, down there I am suffocated.
Long may I fly on my bike.

JUST DIFFERENT

I read things about me,
But it's not me, how can that be me?
But then I know it is.
Reading the things about me is like looking in the mirror and not knowing who
the other man is who looks back at me;
The things that I do are written on paper but erased from my mind,
I'm living so many lives in one lifetime
And I think that I'm lucky.
We don't remember to breathe and yet we do,
I don't remember doing and yet I have done.
It's not all bad, it's just different.

MAIN ACTIVITIES SINCE THE PUBLICATION OF THE BOOK:

1. "Slow Puncture" has been accepted by the American based organisation, AlzAuthors, a "volunteer-run organisation that works with authors to connect caregivers with the best books and blogs about Alzheimer's…"

2. The Universities of Hull, Bangor and Essex have all used "Slow Puncture" for their students' dementia studies courses.

3. We have made podcasts with Pippa Kelly, Penny Bell, The Bold Age, Rosanna Miles, Deepness Dementia Radio, Marianne Sciucco (AlzAuthors), Lori La Bey (AlzSpeaks), Jennifer Fink (Fading Memories) and Dementia Carers Count. Peter did a live presentation for Care UK and had an online chat with Tour de France winner Geraint Thomas in conjunction with The Alzheimer's Society.

4. Peter and I were invited to be the guests for an online event hosted by AlzAuthors in conjunction with "Hilarity for Charity". This charity is the brainchild of 'A' listed actor Seth Rogen and his partner, Lauren Miller.

5. The book has appeared several times in the top 100 books on Amazon in the category of memoirs and medical biographies.

6. We are currently giving presentations on the book and living well with dementia to various Suffolk libraries, social care organisations and financial institutions.

7. We have appeared on BBC Look East, on BBC Radio Suffolk and in The East Anglian Daily Times as well as in cycling magazines and a range of dementia organisations' websites.

8.   Peter's chosen charity is Alzheimer's Research UK. In September, Teresa, Peter, Andrew and I cycled from London to Suffolk and raised over £1,200 for the charity.

9.   "Slow Puncture" is now on its second print run, published by The Book Guild and available on Amazon, Waterstone's, The Book Depository and other good bookshops. It is also available in a Kindle version.

THE STORY BEHIND THE FRONT COVER

Some time ago, Peter was involved in the award winning Channel Four documentary, "The Restaurant That Makes Mistakes". During that time, he met Sue Strachan and her partner, Sheila Marsh. Emerging, phoenix-like from the burned embers of the restaurant (joke: it didn't burn), a friendship was born and has been sustained despite the geographical distances between the friends.

Artist, Sheila, offered to create and draw the front cover of this book: you can see the shadowy figure of Peter, clutching a butterfly net, trying to capture those elusive words. And, of course, given his years of work in the timber trade, the forest environment is particularly significant for Peter. I believe that the cover represents more than just a book cover: it shows the importance of Peter's working life, the enduring impact of friendships and, perhaps more poignantly of all, that light can still shine through the darkness that is dementia.

Thank you, Sheila, for your time and your artwork.

Peter Berry

Suffolk man, Peter, owned a successful timber business but when he received the diagnosis of early onset dementia, the business was forced to close down. Peter splits his time between cycling around the countryside and giving local and national inspirational talks about how to live well with dementia. Peter is married to Teresa and they have one daughter, Kate.

Deb Bunt

Deb moved to Suffolk three years ago and almost immediately met Peter in the local cycle shop. In helping him write "Slow Puncture", Deb achieved her lifelong ambition to be a published writer. When Deb isn't cycling with Peter and Teresa, she spends her time trying unsuccessfully to shake off her addiction to Arsenal Football Club. Deb is married to Martin and they have two grandchildren.

Daniel Ruffles

Based in Aldeburgh, Suffolk, Daniel is a self-taught landscape photographer with a love of the Suffolk coastline. Daniel has a passion for the great outdoors and never tires of those early morning starts to capture the beautiful colour and mood that the vast landscape offers him.
Daniel's photography lends itself to telling a story beyond the frame, creating familiarity and a sense of place. Daniel's work has featured in both local and major publications, along with being displayed in local galleries in Suffolk.

Printed in Great Britain
by Amazon

81213834R00049